Where To Start?

Writings By:
Tommie L. Stanfield III

To Eddie,
Thank you for the love and support!
I really appreciate you!

Dedication

This book is dedicated to my brother Dennis M. Stanfield. He introduced me to poetry without physically telling me. He dropped secret hints for me that I picked up within his poetry, which showed me that there is an outlet in writing. His passion for writing pushed me to give it a try, and fell in love with it. All in all, he is the reason why I am writing.

Denpoet

He wrote about his struggle, his journey, his love, and his dreams
He's always been with us, he never switches teams
He stays true to his poetry
Well because he is poetry
It is one with him, so he just let it take control and write for him
But using his mind that may take him on a whim
His poetry is so influential like Stevie is to him
So I began my journey into writing
He helped me to understand that I should just let it go instead of fighting
I let it control me and now I can't stop writing
5 books with 70 plus in each book
His mind is so complex, thoughts he just lets them cook
And the product is as pure as a great poet
Which he is
So it's nothing I can say but I'm glad that he's my brother
He helped me enter into this realm of poetry that I think no other could
Will I be able to get through the trees of his mind or be lost in the woods?

Table of Contents

Where To Start:
I. The Beginning Of

The Beginning of The End

The beginning of the end
Beginning of something great
The end of something dull
I want to feel the best feelings of the beginning
But never the bittersweet taste of the end
I want to stay toward the beginning
And stay away from the end
I want to feel the motivation and the excitement of
the beginning
I don't want to feel the disappointment and
dissatisfaction of the end
I want to enjoy the feelings of the beginning
But the feeling of fear of the end is in the back of
my mind
But I can't be afraid of the end because everything
comes to an end
Let's end the fear of the end
And begin the feeling of hope

Observing

I guess you can say I've always learned from other
people
I try not to put myself in certain positions
And doing that doesn't make me "cool"
But I follow my own path
Don't listen to what other people have to say
because it's mostly negative
Stay to myself, who's better to trust than yourself
That's why I don't fully open up to people
I have trust issues, never fully trusting in anyone
Other people's experiences are how I learn
If I see something I don't like about somebody
I'm not going to be a hypocrite and do the same
things
I'm going to change for the better
I learned from other people
That I shouldn't get mad over what someone says
Because if I react, they are winning
I try not to let anything get to me
So I stay quiet
Always have been and probably always will be
But that doesn't mean I won't speak what's on my
mind
But if it's not going to make the situation better
Then why say it
As I sit back and watch

I just make mental notes on what I want for my life
and what I don't
People always say that I'm too nice and why don't I
get mad
I treat people the way I want to be treated, even
though most of time they don't return the favor
And I don't let things get to me
I'm still maturing but I know what I want for my
life
And playing games isn't what I want

Lesson Learned

Yes care about what people say
Especially if they talking about you
Let their comments tear you down
To the point where you need more than tape to put
you back together
Let their words seek into your skin
And live inside of you
Really pay attention to their words
And take all of them to heart
Let your mind, soul, and body break down
Really pay attention to every emotion that you feel
when you hear or read those things
Now since that has happened
You learned a valuable lesson

What Happened?

Where are the people
That would sacrifice everything for the betterment
of others
Everybody is selfish nowadays
Ain't no favors unless you bringing something to
the table to exchange
It's all about what can I get out of this for myself
No more favors just to be friendly
Expecting nothing in return
Rather than helping you out
I'd rather see you burn
I see you struggling right now
What can I do to help
Let me help you get through the situation that
you're in
But in exchange for the help
When I call you, you better pick up
But when you slip up and ask for help
The other person remembers when you didn't help
Now that's a shame
Where are the people
That would sacrifice everything for the betterment
of others

Spreading Love

I thought we were supposed to be spreading love
All I see is hate and envy
People killing other people and other people
becoming enemies
Fake love up close and shots from afar
Negativity gets people nowhere
But when positivity is sought out, we can get
somewhere, anywhere, everywhere
Only with hate and despise, people will be infected
But why not affect people with love
And with all the other stuff reject it
So we can become reconnected to old people that
we use to mess with
And have a positive effect that shows people that
responding with love is affective

Follow Your Heart

If I ever betray my heart
I want it to let me know
And set me straight
Because I want to listen to it
And since it's special to me
I want to always follow it
Lead me where you want me to go
If I choose to follow my heart
I will be going in the right direction
Because the heart is usually right

Fear

What if I'm like this my whole life
Scared, lost, and confused
Not knowing what people would do
Some people have a short fuse
Thinking "I'm not good enough"
Would people be amused
To see another kid chasing a dream but it ended up
being another ruse
I'm trying to follow rules and meet expectations but
failing
I'm trying to walk down this path that was laid out
for me but I lost my balance and can't find a railing
So I'm holding onto nothing
People keep calling me out, and most of the time I
be bluffing
I wonder will these drugs take away the fear, or will
I end up like David Ruffin
So how do I take away the fear without risking my
life
Or is life and fear parallel where you can't have one
without the other
But I guess I'll choose life for the sake of my
mother
And the rest of my family

Because this life is so crazy
I wonder why I'm so lazy
I wonder will I break out of this phase
So much pressure on my back to always get all A's
I wonder if I fail, will I still get those open arms

Lust

This started not because we were cool with each
other
I wanted her body and she wanted mine too
She was open to suggestion so what was I suppose
to do
I wanted her around me
And she wanted to be on top
How was I suppose to say no when she's looking so
good coming out of the water?
I'm willing to sacrifice, yea I'm willing to be the
martyr
I'm taking one for the team but it's really for myself
And I mean it's for her too
I'm just here to help
If it wasn't for my lust then I wouldn't have even
dealt with her
But look at her now, she's trying to take my belt
with her
Not caring where we were, she always wanted me
to play with her
I couldn't stop because she had a hold on me
I was a fiend that kept feeding into the lust
There was no solid foundation, so there was no
trust
We both were using each other as tools
Just ways of feeling good

Love

This started because we were cool with each other
I wanted her mind and she wanted mine too
She was open to suggestion so what was I suppose
to do
I wanted her around me
And she wanted the same
She was looking for somebody real that wasn't with
the games
Had a great mind and a few of other things
We always talked and had a good time
She was always telling other people "he's mine"
She was very protective and that put things in
perspective
That she really cared for me
Cared about my well-being and always prayed for
me
I think she's a keeper
I'm trying to get deeper in this relationship
It's been a couple years now
And I'm really thinking if I should lock her down
I think she's ready and willing
To be with me and all my feelings
Trying to get me out my shell, so she's continually
peeling
I want this forever, forever feeling this feeling

Fear of Lust

I really want to do this
But at the same time, I'm still not sure
I want to give you something that's just so pure
I'm gone be at my purest when we married
If we do this now, there's no telling for our future
and that is scary
But I don't want to lose you
But I don't want to lust for you
What if it was just one time
But after that you start getting comfortable
With the cycle that could be created
Mindlessly lusting for each other
I think it's time for a break
But you want to keep going, life is too short to wait
There's no feelings so if you don't want to do this
anymore, we could end it
But I'm fighting with my body because it wants to
stay
But my mind is telling me go, you'll be an addict if
you stay
I want one last time then I'll leave
But that wasn't the last time, I was deceived

Fear of Love

I really want to do this
But at the same time, I'm still not sure
I want to give you something that's just so pure
I don't know when I'll be at my purest
Maybe it's never
I really want to be with you
But I don't want you getting comfortable
Next thing you know, you saying you love me
I'm sorry that you said that because I don't know
what that is
Sorry to break your heart but I don't know what I
can give
Maybe it's more space if you are feeling like that
I'm so scared of loving because I get too attached
Then it will take a while for me to bounce back

Not Your Fault

People should never blame themselves for
something somebody else has done
Don't let them get out of the situation thinking that
they won
Keep your head up and keep thinking that you're
the one
Because it's true
Nobody can take the joy away from you
It just takes time to heal
It's still there despite what you feel
Don't let anybody tell you how to feel
Don't let anybody ruin you
Because it's not your fault

Clear My Mind

I want to clear my mind, and put myself in a better place
I want to say I'm still out of this world but I been landed, no longer in outer space
I want to keep my circle small, but it still requires a lot of space
I try to take care of people, even when we're not face to face
I want people to realize this life is not a race
It's not about first, second, or third
As long as you make it to the point where your voice can be heard
Don't let them keep you trapped like a caged bird
But it's like I'm trapped inside my own mind
Looking for a door that I can't seem to find
It's like I'm rejecting freedom
But I want the liberty of being free
But how can I get out of my own head
It's something that is a part of me

Misplaced

Honestly I feel like I'm in the wrong generation
I don't act or feel like I belong
In this generation where everybody thinks they
know everything
Where there are people being ruined because of cut
throat people
People that just do things with no reasoning
People that don't care about each other
A generation where having feelings for someone is
just a phase
Catching feelings is looked at as being soft
Expressing feelings is such a hassle
Having only one girl or dude is not enough
Staying faithful is so difficult
Telling the truth is so hard
Lies only lead to more hurt
Cheating is just such a common thing
A generation where people are talking less and pay
attention to their phones more
People think revenge is better than letting go
It's all about the get back
He hurts you, so you find a way to hurt him more
People caring about their own pride and ego more
than a person they hold close

They would rather have something worse happen
then admit they were wrong
People only looking out for themselves
It's just that I think differently than everyone else
Which I see as a good thing

Detachment

Why even get close to people
Eventually they'll be gone like the wind
They'll never look back
So don't wait on it
Thinking that nobody cares
Is more soothing than thinking people care
Then later to find out they don't, is hard to bear
So don't get close because soon they'll fly away
Don't stop them because you might be the shade
keeping them from seeing their brighter day

Back Stage

I want to be heard
But never seen
Being in the open has never been me
And if people look hard enough
They would come to see
Me behind the scenes
Instead of on the big screens
In the shadows like the dark knight
With invisible wings, so no one can see me take
flight

Attachment

It's just a feeling when you vibe with someone
Just being good friends, you feel like you belong ·
Maybe feeling a feeling that you haven't felt in so
long
Just wanting it forever, a life long friend
Someone willing to bend over backwards just to
make sure you're good
Somebody that's willing to go through the fire with
you
And still continue on
Trying to prolong for so long because this is hard to
find
That someone's hard to find
That special bond has to be deeply rooted
And if it's not, then that friendship can be swiftly
ruined
But with that special attachment, nothing can be
done to leave them in ruins

Distinction

How do you recognize the real from the fake?
How would you know if they are telling the truth or
just lying?
Really being sincere or deceitful
Why can't everybody just...
Wait, that's asking for too much
Trying to cut the grass to find all the snakes
But sometimes you still don't see them
Trusting people is hard
Who really has your best interests
And will we ever find out
Keeping the circle small doesn't get rid of leeches
Because the closest friends can be the leeches
And sometimes we still don't learn, even though
they teach us
That they aren't in it for our best interest
That ruins it for the people that are actually trying
to help you out
They don't have an ulterior motive
They're the motivation to improve yourself
But sometimes it's hard to tell the difference

Mask

Tragic events can break strong people
People that you didn't even think could be broken
But sometimes it's just a matter of time
Your life can be of constant struggle
But they never know because your constantly in a
good mood
Putting on a mask is a very frequent thing now
Even I do it
Hidden emotions, never really coping so you're
Constantly choking on the thoughts that's in your
head
Not telling anyone, keeping to yourself
It's not good, it's actually bad for your health

Inspiration

Give me the passion of Kendrick
And the soul of Cole
And the Determination of both
Let me be the Change I want to see
And let it be 4 Your Eyez Only
And keep the Money Trees to yourself
Nobody need to know how much u got
Cause you might get robbed because it's a Cole
World
So I bought this sweater to Warm Up
But now I only have a Dollar and a Dream
And because of my Complexion I have to think of
ways to scheme
Because what can you get For Free?
Nothing, so I got to make enough Just To Get By
I'm just a good kid that's wondering How High his
ceiling is
Until then I'll Levitate
I Welcome all Love and deny the hate
Now watch this Black Boy Fly through the city just
to Runaway
Writing a Note to Self and everyone else that I just
can't Stay
In this Land of the Snakes

Apparently people can't be trusted
So I got you Cut You Off now
Can't let them see me Breakdown because they
might think I'm soft
I don't care though, I'm just trying to Balance the
good and evil
Staying away from the Badness because their ways
are deceitful
I am a Born Sinner that never idolizes False
Prophets
People praising Dead Presidents, man yall got to
stop it
It's Now or Never and the choice is yours
Have faith and accept God's Gift
Or be another one of the Lost Ones chasing Mo
Money
You got to be swift, and avoid the Trouble

Tradition

We're here to carry on tradition
Sitting around the old heads, just listen
To the old tales and wise words
Listen how they slur their verbs
As the young generation we have a responsibility
To carry on these traditions continually
The old owls hand down what can't be handed
It's not a ship to be landed
Its stories and glory passed on
It's a family group we all join
The tradition of different families and cultures
We have to protect it or it's attacked by vultures
It's the family gatherings and foods cooked
Tradition is the values booked
Me and Tom plan to carry on tradition

By: Dennis M. Stanfield

Where To Start:
II. My/Our Story

Comfortable

I love everything about me
From the brown skin to the bright personality
Love the skin and people with similar color should love it too
I don't want to be any other color because I'm comfortable in my skin
To me, being black is a win
My culture is so vast
History is really important to me
And the fact that we don't get credit for it is ridiculous
Lies are being told about my people and I don't want to hear that
Truth is spoken from our people but they don't want to hear that
No matter what anybody says, I'm comfortable in my skin
To me, being black is a win
We are all the same, even to God, because we all sin
He made me this way, so I should be proud of my color
I am a couple shades darker than my mother
But we both still love the Sun and the melanin

Nobody can tell me black is nothing, because I'm
comfortable in my skin
To me, being black is a win
Black is beautiful
I can't say it in any other way
People are running from their color, but not me
because I want to stay
This color forever, even through the adversities
Because it makes me stronger than Hercules
All black people say it with me, I'm comfortable in
my skin
To me, being black is a win!

Our Story

People should wish everybody well
Because being black, we never knew when we're
going to hear the bell
Then we know we about to fight
There are few W's and a lot of L's
Because of disadvantages
They even scared of us on college campuses
Clutching their purses harder when we're on the
same elevator
I'm trying to get to the penthouse like you
I'm trying to do what you do but better
But they're forcing me to do more steps
I'm trying to get the same things you want
It's just easier for you
I'm just the sacrifice laying down the bunt, so we
can get a score
But the game is already rigged
So what are we playing for?
Losing in a race because of our race
We're always on the run because they want to chase
While our health is on 50
Theirs are on 110
So their thinking "how can we not win"
Let's just send them niggers back on a boat
And poof, we're gone like the wind

But without us, they wouldn't have a lot
But they don't think about that
They just think about the plot to get rid of us
But we're not going anywhere
All odds against us because life ain't fair
We started on top
Then they dragged us to the bottom
While we worked hard they were just chilling
They call us the bad guys but the racists are the real villains
Whipping us, spraying us using water hose
Keeping us broke not being able to afford old clothes
Had us working in the field
And even today being shot and killed, in these streets
Videos are being shown
But no conviction
This is real life but they treat it like science fiction
Claiming that we're the monsters
But these white people started this gangster stuff, they were the mobsters
Even today, these racists still trying to stomp us
But nah, Obama was in the white house and they thought life was over
But now that Trump is in the office, so I'm thinking "do I really want to be sober"

But I got to be, no I have to be
I got to be performing some magical stuff like it's alchemy
Because this black magic is real, it's something that you got to see
The black man that I am, I don't care if anyone else is, but I'm proud of me

Do I Make You Nervous?

Yea I noticed how you kept looking back as I
walked behind you
Do I make you nervous?
Is it because of my color?
Of course it is because you listen to the stereotypes
So you don't know which ones are "good" or "bad"
So you stay safe and assume all
So you decide to either speed up or slow down
Oh, he's acting like he dropped something
Smart move, now you're behind me
But what if I volunteer to help would you turn me
around or accept the help?
He says no thank you
So I keep walking
But you're still not safe
So you look some more for something that you
won't find
But you lost me so that's good enough

Uncomfortable

Why is that a person of a certain race is not
comfortable being surrounded by another race?
Black people feel uncomfortable in white
neighborhoods
White people feel uncomfortable in black
neighborhoods
These preconceived mind states are ruining people
Sometimes the non-comfortability turns violent
Where one race shoots the other because of the
preconceived notions or stereotypes
Or the police get called because of no
comfortability
Then the guns get pulled because they're afraid,
trying to protect themselves

Stranger

I'm walking down the street with my cousin
We're in a different neighborhood, so my senses
are buzzing
I feel people are watching us because of the skin
color
The fact that we're darker than peanut butter
And them, they're lighter than a stick of butter
They make assumptions
All the odds against us, so how are we able to
function
As we walk, I'm thinking "how can this change?"
By continuing to push through the injustices
But it's like we're strangers in our own land
We're treated like foreigners in our own land
Keeping us down and discouraging us from making
our own brand
We're just adding some flavor to this country,
that's bland
But we either get the hand or the book thrown at us
Even though we're like them, citizens but they treat
us like strangers
Lower class than them, that's why they're nervous
when I pass
Because I'm a stranger to them that doesn't have
any class

Question

Question
Why do I get accused first?
I wasn't even in the situation
Wanting to see my ID for identification
And when the gun comes out, I'm thinking why me?
But he doesn't understand at all
I'm just here for my education
But I'm stuck in a bad situation
Right now I'm facing a cop with a gun
Not knowing if I'll die tonight or if I'll be able to see the sun
Or if I will live long enough to see my first son
Or if I will live long enough to graduate college
Or if I will live long enough to continue working on my brain gathering knowledge
Or if I will live long enough to go home
I've always wanted to go since I was a kid
Actually being there instead of watching these vids
Being involved in the culture up close and personal
But will I even make it through tonight, I don't even know

Stereotypes

Yes, I have been racially profiled
Because of my skin and my stereotypical style
They see me as an enemy because of my niggerish
crowd
You better be careful with them because they wild
Walking around the mall
Got people thinking "what is he going to steal?"
Or is he going to sexually assault someone
Trying to cop a feel
But nah, that's not me
All I'm trying to do is chill
But I can't because people are always watching my
every move
So I have to move carefully
Or I won't be waking up the next morning to hit
snooze

Keeping Us Down

They want us shackled again
But nah, never again
We not taking what they hand us anymore
We're taking what they don't want us to see
So they making different rules to keep us away
And if we don't, we're going to prison
The modern-day slavery where we can't escape
Or sending us to the grave
But then we're just following their blueprint
They're doing everything they can
To keep us like crabs in a barrel
Threatening us with our eyes looking down the cold
barrel
That can turn hot in less than seconds
Or they got the batons out
Until we're out cold
We can't do nothing but fold
Because we fear for our lives
But our stories will still be told

Obstacles

Today, we are whipping cars around
Back then they were whipping dogs
And we were whipping them around
Pushing numbers for floors for them
Following their directions
But we got our own direction
So when we look back, reflection
We know we were free
To make our own decision
And when we look at the revision
We see the mistakes and do the right thing
And when it's legendary, we put it in writing
Let's not indulge in their entertainment by fighting
Let's stick together and never break
Out of focus for our aspirations and dreams
And pay attention to this world because it's not
what it seems
They setting us up for failure
Trying to stop us from being Kings and Queens
And great things that we are and will be

Us vs. Them

We march, we stand, we sit, we run
They spit, they disrespect, they chase
We're unarmed, they're armed
We're beaten, they're not phased
We fight, they use weapons
We're harmed, they're armed
We're heavily injured, they could care less
We call out for help, they ignore us
We call out for help, they hear us but don't listen
We call out for help, they beat us
We call out for help, they help us to make little
progress
We call out for help, they give no help, so no
progress
We make one small step, they kick us back three
steps
We cry, they laugh
We struggle, they laugh
We protest, they laugh
We protest, they laugh
We protest, they yell "Get back!"
We protest, they fight us
We love, they spite us
We live, they smite us with their hands, feet, and
weapons
We just want respect

Old/New Mind State

I don't appreciate what you've done to me
Forcing me to set the table but having me eat
outside without cutlery
Like I'm an animal or maybe a savage beast
But they barely feed the animals even though they
have a feast
While I worked, they drank tea in peace
Had me working with no pay
With no pay!
How is that legal?
But I don't know of any legalities or formalities
Because of no education
I should be taught, I want to learn
But they don't want to see that, they would rather
have me crash and burn
So I'll escape and follow the north star
I don't even know what state I'm in
So I don't know how far I should even go
But I can't think about that now because I don't
know if I'll even survive today
But that's how it is today, all work and no play, I
mean rest
But what do I know, my master knows best

They Do/Don't Want

What would people say if he died today
Knock on wood
Nah, he can only hope and pray
Who would be devastated that this educated young
man died so young
Would they be surprised if white masks were
surrounding this man as he hung
Would it start a civil war or has it already begun?
All he had was some skittles, was it a cell phone or
maybe a toy gun
Everybody want to be black but when it comes
down to it
It ain't no fun
They only want the good things
They don't want to be discriminated against
They don't want to be profiled
They just want to have dark skin and more style
They want the hair but they don't want to bear the
burden that comes with it
They act like us and they get famous
We act like us and we still nameless
Not that we want the limelight but we just want to
shine bright like the stars in the sky
All we try to do is fly

But they beat us and break our wings
And shoot down our dreams
And only show us darkness and make it seem like
it's a bad thing
Trying to keep us in the sunken place
So they can run us and run things
Walk all over us like we're not human beings
You and I are the same
Why can't you see that?
Maybe your eyes are set to turn red when you see
brown or black
And green or blue when you see your own
And they see us as the needy so they sometimes
throw us a bone
But we don't need it because we fend for ourselves

Struggles

Some people complain that life ain't fair
But other people that are using food stamps don't care
As long as they're putting food on the table
And several other families are not being able, to do the same
And some rich people just think it's a game
Seeing who can make the most money and competing for fame
I feel we all should be paid the same
Man, the struggle is real
People not having enough money to get a meal
They can't find a good deal
So their only option is to starve or steal
And that's not what they want for they're life
I am here to reveal the struggle
It's not as appealing as it is on TV
It's worse
It makes you want to burst into tears
And its been happening for years
But people still ignoring it like it's not an issue
It's so bad out there, people are crying, go get them a tissue

And more of what they need
Living off of minimum wage, they don't have
enough to feed their family, but they got to make it
work

Equal

We have to form a new mind state
That couldn't in any way shape or form increase the
crime rate
Black people are more than what they say and
that's our fate
So don't let anyone say different
Because to them, we're all the same
So we should stand united against those people
Make them see the bigger picture instead of their
usual perspective, through their peephole
Because we are people, just like everyone else
But we don't get the same treatment because we're
looked at as not equal

From The Dreamer, To The Dream

From the dreamer, to the dream
From Martin Luther King, to Barack Obama
From the dreamer, to the dream
From slavery, to the white house
From the dreamer, to the dream
We used to dream the dream
And now we have lived the dream

Black is Beautiful

Nobody can tell me black isn't beautiful
People should never be ashamed of what the skin
color is
Whatever it is, take pride in it
Show them that "I'M BLACK AND I'M PROUD"
Thanks to James Brown and the other musicians at
Motown
Showing people that being black is nothing to be
ashamed of
Showing people that #blacklivesmatter isn't a
movement that is against white people
But a movement to make black lives better
Protecting our families from the danger that's been
going on for over 30 years
We were sitting and now standing against these
injustices
With all the odds against us, we need to stand
united
For something that we all believe in
And never forget that
Black is beautiful
God created black people
And God doesn't make mistakes

Black Queen

There are plenty of black women that shows you
black don't crack
So let me tell you, I want that
A strong black woman can propel your life forward
She shows black excellence and that's a direction
that I want to go toward
I want her to be my future, my last, my everything
We can show the world that being black is
everything
We need more black relationships that is in it for
the long term
Like Cliff and Claire, Martin and Gina, Dwayne
and Whitley, and Phil and Vivian
These black relationships on TV were killing em
Those characters showed the chase to marriage and
the love of marriage
Everything I want, but not scripted
Showing other people that black people are gifted
Instead of these stereotypical relationships, we need
to shift it
To more loving, understanding, and faithful
relationships
That turns into more that would require us to meet
the other's kin folk

Growing old together, still laughing at the same jokes
Enjoying each other even in the bad times when we want to choke, each other but we don't because we need, love, and care for each other
This black Queen should be able to take care of me better than my mother
And I'll return the favor
Even growing up, chocolate has always been my favorite flavor
But I want my special chocolate woman that I can savor

Where To Start: III. With Her

Past

She fell out of the sky
She might be an angel
A human in disguise
But without the halo
She's a Queen that was hurt
She's trying to refrain from being like what her man
became
So she left him
Not wanting to feel that same way again
But it's always in the back of her mind
Looking for a good replacement, which is not easy
to find
The next shouldn't be because of the ex
And just the sex shouldn't be the reason for the next
It's no need, it's over, why would you even flex?
Just leave it alone and let the ex be the ex
He's the past and you're a Queen
Looking for a man that is nothing less than King
You can't get the full course meal if you keep trying
to get wings
But why keep trying to talk you up when you're not
even listening

Trust Issues

"I'm not like the others"
"I'm different"
People can't even use these to be sincere anymore
Because people abuse them
They say it and end up being like every other
person
Messing with people's head just to get what they
want
And once they get it
They gone, never to be heard from again
But then again, they may find the one that's sincere
and respectful
But after a while they get bored and neglectful
And start messing with other people, ignoring their
relationship, so disrespectful
Trying to keep the late nights quiet
Phone is lighting up, but he or she's not by it
Making up an excuse for the message, but the other
doesn't buy it
Living with trust issues, but trying to deny it

Work in Progress

Living in a generation where cheating is the norm
Having side chicks is common
Or maybe it's more in the open now
If somebody is willing to be in a relationship
There is no reason you should be messing with
other people, like how
Do you expect people to trust you when you're
lying?
Then you get bored of your relationship and just
stop trying
That's what really messes people up
They have trust issues
And their hearts are broken
Trying to pick up the pieces without any help
Every man that comes around
She thinks he's about the same thing as her ex
Just looking at her as a piece of meat, just for sex
So when you see him in the streets
You have a right to flex, right?
I'm thinking, nah baby girl just give it a rest
If he did you wrong
Ignore him, he's out of your life
Live your life how you want it
Not just to stunt on him

Starting Over

Starting over is scary
You gave your all for the last person
And then there was the break up
It lasted a couple years
And it was ended in a blink of an eye
All the progress lost
Sometimes you wish it was a game
That you could just return to the checkpoint
But nah, life is different
Because you'll have to restart the whole game
And play with a new character, person
All the things that you once had is no more
All you have is knowledge
That you can apply to this new game
The path is going to be different
So there is no speeding through to reach the point
you were once at
Just going to have to forget about that
But it's hard though
Thinking about the different aspects of the previous
game
Will the new character be as good as the old
character?
Or will the character be worse

What if we don't make it as far
Doubt always resurfaces
There's no getting rid of it
So you just hit snooze
For it to come back and bug you again later
Trying to take things slow but you made it so far
before, why not try to speed things up a little bit

Looking From a Distance

I apologize for the distance
But I'm in a place that's safe to me
I'm selfish for only thinking of myself
So I guess I'll ask, what you want us to be?
Just friends or are you looking for something more?
Full disclosure, I'm not really into the night life
I rather chill and have a drink with my soon to be
wife
Oh, you're not the one, I guess that's fine
So I'm still searching for the one that I hope I can
find
Looking for someone who won't blow up in my
face
And if she's the right one, I am willing to chase
But until then, I'm fine with my space

Digging

Let me dissect your mind and jump into eyesight
Let me see what you have seen and all the wrong
you've committed in hindsight
And let me delete them out of your mind because
the past can't be right
So you can finally shine bright like you always
wanted to
And forget all those people that didn't believe in
you
Let me confide in you
I'm the someone that you can tell all of your secrets
to
I believe in you
I'm the someone that wants to show you something
new
Through these lines, I want to show you that I'm
special too
To you and all the people around you
What do you aspire to be?
Let the negative energy perspire out of you like
you're baking in the hot sun
What can you find in me?
What do you see in me?
I only want the truth because it's something that is
needed

Would you let me go with an open wound,
bleeding?
Or would you patch me up and then continually
keep beating?
Or would you patch me up and then consider
leaving?
Or would you patch me up and then stay?
I want to know your way of thinking
I wonder if you start lying, do you profusely start
blinking
What are your worst memories?
If you talk about them, then that could be your
remedy
It's not good to keep it on the inside
Don't be afraid to show feelings, get rid of your
foolish pride
Because that's getting you nowhere fast
Tell me more about yourself, details for your future
and about your past

Rushing

That is the perfect depiction
She doesn't really know that she's my prescription
Maybe I can go as far as saying she's my addiction
Because I need her at least once a day
But the thing is that she is a walking reenactment of
my last
So I just assume that we can zoom pass the old stuff
and pick up where I left off
But that would be moving kind of fast
But slow isn't how I want to take it since I know
you so well
We belong together, so I know we won't fail

Take The Shot

Building up your confidence saying "I'm the one"
But how can you be so sure that she's the chosen
one
He takes a shot to get rid of fear
He approaches her and asked her a couple of
questions
He got her laughing and they exchange numbers
They've been talking for a while so he decided to
ask the question
She answered…

The Start

I wasn't looking for anything
But she was thinking differently
I mean we just clicked so perfectly
Then I was thinking why not, right?
Spending time together would be great
And she was cute too
But anyway, we started hanging out
Our feelings were mutual
And our bond was so deep
We jumped in the pit together
Fearless with both feet

She's Beautiful

She's beautiful without trying
She's beautiful on the inside
She's beautiful on the outside
She's beautiful when she wants to be
I'm never going to set her free

She's beautiful when she doesn't care
She's beautiful with her short hair
She's beautiful with a little crazy
She's beautiful with personality
Her beauty is my reality

She's beautiful with her bonnet on
She's beautiful with her mask on
She's beautiful when she wakes up
She's beautiful with a great mind
And I'm glad to say that she's all mine

The Only One

If she is the one
She is the ONLY one
There is no other
And that's a promise
When I'm with her
There are no others
Only her
She's all I see
She's all I want
So she shouldn't even think about me replacing her
Because there is no replacement
No woman can replace who I have in my clutches
I fell so hard
She got me in crutches
But in the end
She is mine and I am hers

Technology

Technology is such a great thing
But not when it comes to us
Cell phones are terrible
She's always distracted
She's all worried about her social media life
She's forgetting I'm even in the room
I complain when she's on her phone
I don't want her on the phone but she's attached to it
I want her to be as attached to me as that phone
Or is that asking for too much?

"I Love You"

At first, I love you is said with so much feeling
So much emotion
But when does saying that just become redundant
And you're just saying it for the sake of saying it
Where is the feeling?
Where is the emotion?
Where's the real love?
Where did it go?

Overthinking

He tends to over think everything based off of
Her behavior
Her body language
Her facial expression
He tends to question his actions
What am I doing wrong?
What am I not doing?
What would happen if I did this?
He tends to question her
Where have you been?
What have you been doing?
Who have you been out with?
Why don't you love me anymore?

"We Need to Talk"

Whenever she says that
It's nothing good
He already knew what was coming
But she tried to postpone it like it's nothing
But it was more than nothing
And they both knew it
It's over
Now she's blaming herself
She just wasn't ready for a relationship
He's just sitting quietly
He knew it was coming but it was still a shock
She's trying hard not to drop tears
What would you do if she started crying?
All he could do was try to process
It felt like it just started
And things were going so well

Memories Part I

Just sitting here thinking
About her and what could've been
But if I had her
Would that truly be a win?
Well I guess I'll never find out
The most I can do is imagine
But I can't be stuck on her
I got to move on
But the memory is stuck in my head
Having fun when I'm with her
And thinking about her when we depart
All the good times we had
But just being with her was my favorite part
It was too early to tell but with more time
She could've had my heart
But things just happened to go the other way

Letting Go

He's kind of giving up
But still wanting her more
She's like a drug
That's too good to ignore
Once he gets attached
He doesn't want to let go
But sometimes they force him to
Or he feels like he has to

Maybe Not Forever

She said she wanted this forever
But before forever even came
She was done
It's sad she didn't even want to stick out there until
the end
But why expect that
She's still young with a lot of life to live
Why stop her
Despite of what he feels
He can't be selfish

Memories Part II

He wants her
But a burden is not what he's trying to be
Constantly on his mind
But he wants her to feel free
To make any choice that she wants
But it's just some things about her
Her smile is so beautiful
Her sense of humor is so stupid but he gets it and
loves it
Her laugh is just so contagious
She just makes him feel like he's famous
If they were in a movie
He would only want those two acting
Nobody else is needed
No distractions
No cuts, only actions
He wants all of her time
Not a single fraction

Where To Start: IV. Ends With God.

First Love

He wants you to come back to Him
Your first love
You have gone astray
You need to find your way back soon
Before it's too late

Believe

Walk by faith and not by sight
So when He comes back, we'll take flight
Reaching new heights that on earth you couldn't
reach
I'm here to talk about Jesus but not to preach
He died on the cross and rose again not to deceive
But to mold us into believers
Believe that He can perform miracles
He's changing your life in ways you don't
understand yet
But you will later on, I'm willing to bet
He loves everything from the tallest human to the
smallest pet
His creations are sacred
But we don't see that because we're engulfed by
hatred
Let's face it, everything and everyone is special and
unique

Listen

When God says change your ways, you need to
hear Him
Stop, listen, and accept wisdom
Get out of your ways because they can become a
prison
Let them become your old ways because for Him
you are living
Always be grateful with what you have and never
stop giving
Because there is always someone in need
If you haven't heard, then listen now because one
of the seven deadly sins is greed
Don't be selfish because you never know if you'll
ever be the one in need
Ending up like Job losing everything, so you'll beg
and plead
For people to help you out in hard times
Listen to God because He will open a door
So walk through so you can see your breakthrough
that would make you fall to the floor

Obey/Follow

Look at what He can do
Look at what He's done already
But we take Him for granted
We shouldn't panic, we should just trust Him
because He can handle it
Pray for the people around you and for yourself so
you can find the perfect fit
Pray for fortune instead of misfortunes
Having lives and not abortions
Start with just a portion
Of time with Him a day
That's all He asks for with the hope that you won't
stray away
From the path that He has for you, just let Him lead
the way
Just try to follow in His footsteps and He will
protect you every step of the way

Blessings

I often use to think what if I wasn't born this way
I could've been lost with no search of the Lord
I could be in all the wrong places at the wrong
times
I could've been born not in my right mind
I could've been born blind
Being lost in this world with no way out
I could've lost everything and lived with no house
I could've been deaf
I could've had asthma having a limited amount of
breathes
I could've been allergic to chicken, no breasts
I could've been going through depression
I could've been in the south going through heavy
oppression
I could've lost friends because of worldly
possessions
I could've lost a brother due to body failures, but
God
I could've been doomed
I even could've died in the womb
But I'm alive so I am blessed

Thankful

Thank you for giving me life
Thank you for my strife
Thank you for being born in my right mind
Thank you for opening doors I couldn't find
Thank you for closing doors I didn't want closed
But you knew it was toxic
Thank you for heartbreak
Thank you for heartache
Thank you for old friends that you got rid of
because they were fake
Thank you for new friends
Even the ones I can't stand
Because they have a purpose but it's too early to
understand
Thank you for trials and tribulations
Thank you for Revelations
Thank you for your sacrifice
Thank you for a grain a rice
Everything that you give will suffice
Thank you for being omnipresent and omnipotent
Thank you for watching over my family and I
Even though I don't deserve it because sometimes
I'm not a perfect guy
Thank you for the win

Thank you for the loss
Thank you for forgiveness of sin
Thank you for paying the cost

"In everything give thanks…" 1 Thessalonians 5:18

Fulfillment

In June when I was 8
Walking in the church feeling good because today
was a special day
The gown was put on me, I was ready to go
They prayed over me then dipped me real slow
Then back up real quick
I was born again feeling like a first-round pick
Later they gave me the mic and I guess I was ready
for the stage
My memory verse is John 3:17 and I recited it with
no help
They asked me "Why do you come to this church?"
I answered, "because God wanted me at this
church"
Everyone gasped and laughed because they thought
that was cute and it was unexpected
Coming from an 8 year old
Such personality, they might have thought I would
be shy and fold
When I walked back to my seat, I couldn't stop
smiling and laughing
I probably didn't fully get what I was happening
But I do now

I gave my life to Jesus and he's always in my heart now
In my mind, in my thoughts, there's no getting him out now
Trying to live my life for Him, I can't possibly let him down now

That Night

I hate that I'm writing this
Cause I don't ever want to relive this night
When I got the phone called we rushed out
And I'm in the car thinking that everything was
alright
Man was I wrong
I got out the car running as fast as I could
When I got there, his body just lying there
The paramedics were doing everything they could
When my dad walked in
He just fell to the ground
I couldn't even see my mom walk in
These tears were blurring my vision
My brother ran from work
He was a man on a mission
It felt like the air was getting thin because it felt
like we all couldn't breathe
Taking deep breathes and claiming everything was
going to be okay
Praying to God that everything is okay
Just thinking why him, why him, why him
And praying to God that everything is okay
Never have I prayed so hard in my life
They couldn't hear or feel anything
1, 2, 3 CLEAR

I almost collapsed
Like no
I wasn't persuasive enough
So I started doubting
Trying to block it
But it wasn't stopping
You could only tell me one thing to stop me from
dropping
1, 2, 3 CLEAR
I never cried so much in my life
But now I'm glad he's okay
Whatever God tells you to do
Just listen and obey
Because He saved my brother's life
And that's a debt I can't ever repay
I just pray this night doesn't constantly show in my
head on replay

Pray

All you can do is pray
Pray for a fast recovery
Pray that you'll make it through
Pray that you'll make it home too
Pray that opportunity is for the taking
Pray that no time is wasted
Pray that your dream will come true as long as you
chase it
Pray that you'll be ready when you come face to
face with
Your fears that have been putting tears in your eyes
Pray for all the truths to come out and no more lies
Pray that He'll protect all of our lives
Pray that motivation always drives you to do better
Pray that you'll get through the situation even
though you knew better
Pray for wisdom
Pray for a loving heart to spread love
Pray for peace
Pray for a piece of mind
Pray for the heart to grind to get where you need to
go
Pray for everyone because we all need it

Doubt

Everybody is saying that He's so great
Since He is, then why would I be worthy of Him
Why do I deserve this treatment
Why am I getting blessed because I am just like
everyone else
Sinning and being of this world
Thinking about myself and nobody else
Thinking of making a lot of money and spending it
on myself
Hanging out with people I shouldn't be
Starting relationships that aren't right for me
Tearing me down mentally and physically
Not praying everyday like I should be
Not thinking before I speak, most of the time ends
miserably
Doing stuff I shouldn't be
Making mistakes I can't retake, how could You be
proud of me
How can I be more like You when there's so much
doubt in me
Not turning to anyone when there were problems
with me
Not even You, but You were still here for me
After all this, I'm stuck thinking
Why would He die for me?

Punishment

God is punishing us because they took land that
wasn't theirs
He's cursing us because we use to be united in His
name
But now we're all divided
In God we trust on the dollar but people only
believe in money
They decided money is material and God and
angels are just fictional
But it's not about what you can touch because the
feeling is spiritual
People may think they're god but, at best, they're
formidable
But if we come back to God, then everything is
forgiven
Start living for Him again, things will get easier
But if not, then the punishment will continue

Chosen One

"The chosen one from the land of the frozen sun" *
Not to quote my brother but he is the chosen one
By God as a testimony to everyone
Recovering from a freak incident like a stroke and a
heart attack
The devil was trying to fight but God was fighting
back
He kept his life protected
The devil tried to take him out but God objected
Gave him breath again
To God's score, we'll add another win
Walking around, even playing basketball again
In his right mind, strength is not all the way there,
but in due time
All we can be is grateful and that's the bottom line

*Lyric by Common: Be (Intro)

All in His Hands

It's no big deal at all, to see me having withdrawals
It's no big deal at all because all I have is God
Encountering transgressions, they're saying that
He's a fraud
He's performing miracles, proclaiming that He is
God
But people only want more, they say that living is
hard
But they won't work for it, there is no fooling God
He knows everything, so there are no secrets
He knows what's going to happen before it happens
He knows you're struggling and He's going to
work it out
It's in progress, just trust His process
Because it will get better, just pray about it, He
promised
Pray without ceasing, let it go, responsibility
decreasing
Taking stress off of your shoulders, how relieving
To see Him work it out and you succeeding
As long as you're believing
He will take over your fights, instead of you
bobbing and weaving
With a chance of getting knocked out
But instead victory is what you are receiving

The Reason

"Keep God first and never forget the order" *
He's the reason for your son or your daughter
Breathing air into their lungs
Showing you that your journey has just begun
Guiding you through your situations
Giving you the motivation
More powerful than the ones that's hating
Don't be stationary, seek Him out
Learn about what He's done with all of His clout
Omnipotent is the word, so believe and He will
show out
Remember everything is on His time
You maybe think you're ready for the mountain
But He says you're not quite ready to climb
Other people could have a whole but you only have
a half
Don't complain because He's the reason you have
all that you have

*Lyric by Maal G: Look To The Sky

Change

You have audacity to challenge me
Even with God on my side, knowing I have the
victory
Positivity is what I want to hear, if not then don't
talk to me
Listen passively because when He speaks and you
listen
Your life will change drastically
Only if you do what He says

FAITH

Darkness, a void we all witness comes in many
forms
From closing your eyes
To being unwise
Going down a road ungodly
Wish he was wise
Mistakes we all make
Isn't it fate?
That's what he thought
He should've fought
The grasp the devil had over his life
He had two kids, and a wife
But the day changed
Feelings built up more contorted than man
Wish he wasn't damned
He had one chance but the materialistic things
shone brighter than his two little kids
The nights out drinking spoke louder than his wife
at home
He'd messed up
As he shouted darling
She wouldn't let up
Gone like sunlight on a cloudy afternoon they left
And so did his purpose
The devil took over

Wish he had a purpose
He found comfort in the drugs
Letting them talk
Little did he know just a few hugs
Would've saved the life he was throwing away
God put us here for a reason
But with the devil in control it was simply treason
Our God is loving
It's not troubling
He needed a bond
Why didn't he listen to John?
He was deep in the void, in need of aid
But in this society today where can you find aid?
The drugs came harder
The devil had power
And in a day
It ended
The devil was splendid
The cries of angels echoed across the sky
Have faith in him
And nothing will come but victories and wins.

"Don't let your hearts be troubled. Trust in God,
and trust also in me."
John 14:1 NLT

By: Zion Rawls

Support

No such thing as a life that's better than yours
Don't envy people because of their life
God gave you your life for a reason
The trial you're in only lasts for a season
God gives the biggest battles to the strongest
soldiers
Even though it's the 10th round and you may think
it's over
Keep going because God got your back
You can take more hits and then keep punching
Even if you take a lost, you'll still be learning
something
We can do all things through Christ, who
strengthens us
With Him on our side, we're unstoppable like a
bus, or a train
Helping us to maintain ourselves through hard
times
The support is beyond anything anyone can give
you
He exceeds all expectations
As long as you practice patience, He will come
through for you

TWMLTH

The false idols of this
World doesn't compare, they
Might try to let you think that if you
Live for Christ, you're making a mistake, but
Through him, all the wrong is taken away, through
Him, all the wrong is forgiven as long as you pray
for forgiveness, can I get a witness?

Thank You

God, none of this would be happening if it wasn't for You.

My family: Mom and Dad, Marc (you started me on this journey), Demetria (helping me with the whole process), Raheem (you got to stay strong and patient, it'll all come back to you), Zion (for the contribution), JaVaughn (for the advice) and the rest of the family.

My Grandparents.

My friends: Navia (for the support and painting the cover) and all of my friends, associates and the people I am not close with.

Thank you to everyone, whether you know it or not, you have been an inspiration to me in one way or another.

End of the Beginning

The beginning is very special to me
But sometimes the beginning must end
But it's definitely not the end

Made in the USA
Columbia, SC
06 November 2024

45518952R00059